Editor
Sara Connolly

Managing Editor
Ina Massler Levin, M.A.

Illustrator
Chuck Ybarra

Cover Artist
Barb Lorseyedi

Art Product Manager
Kevin Barnes

Imaging
Craig Gunnell

Publisher
Mary D. Smith, M.S. Ed.

Author

Sarah Beatty

Teacher Created Resources
6421 Industry Way
Westminster, CA 92683
www.teachercreated.com

ISBN: 978-1-4206-3000-8

©2006 Teacher Created Resources
Reprinted, 2013
Made in U.S.A.

Table of Contents

Introduction

The old adage "practice makes perfect" can really hold true for your child and his or her education. The more practice and exposure your child has with concepts being taught in school, the more success he or she is likely to find. For many parents, knowing how to help their children may be frustrating because the resources may not be readily available.

As a parent it is also difficult to know where to focus your efforts so that the extra practice your child receives at home supports what he or she is learning in school.

Practice Makes Perfect: Dictionary Skills is designed to help practice dictionary skills that are taught in the classroom. The skills appropriate for fourth grade are presented in this book. Most of the words that appear in this book are standard vocabulary, but some special and unusual words are also included.

The following standards or objectives will be met or reinforced by completing the practice pages in this book. These standards and objectives are similar to the ones required by your state and school district. Fourth grade students should be able to do the following:

- The student uses key words, guide words, alphabetical order and indexes to find information for research.
- The student uses dictionaries to find information for research.
- The student uses technology to gather information.
- The student uses a dictionary to define vocabulary words.
- The student identifies the meaning of words in context.
- The student identifies and uses homographs, homophones, and synonyms.
- The student identifies and uses prefixes and suffixes.

Several exercises are provided for the student to practice each skill. They are designed to generate interest and prompt new learning. It is up to the adult to determine which pages are appropriate for his or her student.

An assessment unit at the end of the book reviews the concepts covered throughout the book. This assessment is provided in a standardized-test format to allow students to practice their knowledge as well as their test-taking skills.

How to Make the Most of This Book

Here are some useful ideas for making the most of this book:

- Set aside a specific place in your home to work on this book. Keep it neat and tidy, with the necessary materials on hand.
- Set up a certain time of day to work on these practice pages to establish consistency.
- Keep all practice sessions with your child positive and constructive. If your child becomes frustrated or tense, set the book aside and look for another time to practice.
- Pay attention to the areas in which your child has the most difficulty. Provide extra guidance and exercises in those areas.

To make the most of this book, you will need a dictionary.

Dictionary Terms

Many people would say a dictionary is used to find the meaning of a word. Actually, it can help you do much more. Look at the entry below and read through the many uses of the dictionary.

> **squirrel** skwər-əl n
> a small gnawing animal with a busy tail, soft fur and strong legs for leaping
>
> _____
>
> **word history** comes from the Greek word for squirrel, which was made up from two words. One meant shadow. The other meant tail.

I. Definition

The definition is the meaning of the word. Many words have more than one definition. Each definition is listed and numbered.

II. Spelling

You can use the dictionary to find the correct spelling of a word. It may take some searching, but certain techniques will help you find the word you are looking for. Some words sound alike, so the definition will help you determine if you have found the correct spelling for your word.

III. Pronunciation

Each word listed in the dictionary shows a pronunciation for the word to teach you how to say the word correctly. A pronunciation key will be listed in the front of the book as well as on each page.

IV. Part of Speech

Each definition for the words in the dictionary lists a part of speech. This tells you whether the word is being used as a noun, verb, preposition, conjunction, interjection, adverb, pronoun, or adjective.

V. Word Division

The dictionary shows how to properly divide each word into syllables. This can help with pronunciation and also shows you how to split the word if it must be divided between two lines.

VI. Illustration

Most dictionaries have pictures, especially for unusual words. This will help describe things that may be new or unusual to you.

VII. Word History

Some entries in the dictionary are followed by a word history to explain where the word came from. It will list the language from which the word came, along with its original meaning.

Alphabetical Order

Dictionaries list words in alphabetical order. Using the first letter of each word below, write the words in alphabetical order.

iguana	noun	quarter	grill
paragraph	zipper	eyelash	sidewalk
animal	lilac	unicorn	vegetable
flashlight	caterpillar	toad	drawer
water	jewel	otter	xylophone
helmet	maple	yellow	kingdom
		beach	radish

1. _____

2. _____

3. _____

4. _____

5. _____

6. _____

7. _____

8. _____

9. _____

10. _____

11. _____

12. _____

13. _____

14. _____

15. _____

16. _____

17. _____

18. _____

19. _____

20. _____

21. _____

22. _____

23. _____

24. _____

25. _____

26. _____

Bird Names

The bird names below are all mixed up. Write them again in alphabetical order on the numbered lines. Remember that when words have the same first letter, you need to look at the second letter to determine which comes first.

eagle

crow

osprey

finch

seagull

peacock

starling

oriole

canary

flamingo

pigeon

egret

1. _____

2. _____

3. _____

4. _____

5. _____

6. _____

7. _____

8. _____

9. _____

10. _____

11. _____

12. _____

Filing

Think of the dictionary as having four sections like you might find on a file cabinet. File each word by writing it in the correct section. Make sure each section is in alphabetical order. You will need to use the third letter in each word.

wood	blue	garage	author
straw	rain	aunt	jam
steam	blaze	gadget	ranger
jar	wolf	motor	raft
money	stamp	block	game

ABCD

1. _____

2. _____

3. _____

4. _____

5. _____

MNOPQR

11. _____

12. _____

13. _____

14. _____

15. _____

EFGHIJKL

6. _____

7. _____

8. _____

9. _____

10. _____

STUVWXYZ

16. _____

17. _____

18. _____

19. _____

20. _____

Missing Word

Look at each pair or words. Write a word that comes between the two words alphabetically.
Check a dictionary if you need help.

1. force

    _____

    forgive

2. second

    _____

    sediment

3. base

    _____

    battle

4. lamb

    _____

    lash

5. cape

    _____

    cartoon

6. rare

    _____

    rat

7. kitchen

    _____

    knot

8. monkey

    _____

    moose

9. helmet

    _____

    herb

10. mayor

    _____

    meat

Pick two of the new words you have found and use them in a sentence.

1. _____

2. _____

Finding a Word

Guide words help you find the word you are looking for in a dictionary. The guide word on the top left-hand side of the page is the first word on that page. The guide word on the top right-hand side of the page is the last word listed on that page. Any word in between the two guide words alphabetically will appear on that page.

Use these sample guide words to answer the questions below.

tonight **toucan**	**touch** **traffic**
page 755	*page 756*

1. What is the first word listed on page 756? _____

2. What is the last word listed on page 755? _____

3. On what page would the word *tractor* be listed?_____

4. On what page would the word *torch* be listed?_____

5. What is another word you would find on page 755?_____

6. What is another word you would find on page 756?_____

In the Middle

Look at each pair of imaginary guide words. Put a check (✓) next to the word that would be found on the same page as those guide words.

1. **fish/food**	2. **model/my**	3. **change/curl**	4. **lawyer/license**
— feed	— much	— color	— long
— fly	— mitt	— catch	— left
5. **name/none**	6. **glory/gold**	7. **rang/ring**	8. **hat/high**
— need	— gnu	— reading	— hole
— nut	— grain	— roof	— heel
9. **beet/blend**	10. **ghost/glow**	11. **cheap/coal**	12. **deal/do**
— banana	— guest	— click	— darker
— bird	— giraffe	— cease	— dice

Give Me a C

Which of these imaginary guide word pairs would each word belong under? Write the words under the correct pair.

color	coy	cracker	cowboy
canopy	combine	candle	crab
comic	calves	colony	cheetah
check	cheat	chef	camel

call/cap

_____

_____

_____

cheap/chemical

_____

_____

_____

cow/cream

_____

_____

_____

cold/comment

_____

_____

_____

Absent-Minded Professor

The professor cannot remember where his clothes are! Help him out. Find each word in your dictionary and write the guide words from that page.

1. socks _____ — _____

2. spectacles _____ — _____

3. shirt _____ — _____

4. trousers _____ — _____

5. oxfords _____ — _____

6. vest _____ — _____

7. bow tie _____ — _____

8. blazer _____ — _____

9. overcoat _____ — _____

10. gloves _____ — _____

11. shoes _____ — _____

12. hat _____ — _____

Define This

Once you find a word in the dictionary, you can read its meaning, or *definition*. Sometimes a word has more than one meaning. The most common meaning is listed first and each definition is numbered.

Find and write the correct definition for each underlined word below.

1. The girl jumped over the <u>horse</u> in gymnastics class.

_____

2. The students had a <u>grasp</u> on subjects and verbs.

_____

3. A stream of smoke was coming from the <u>stack</u>.

_____

4. The <u>depression</u> in the road made the car bounce.

_____

5. Rainy days made the boy feel <u>blue</u>.

_____

6. The little girl was a <u>bear</u> when she was tired.

_____

_____

Definition Crossword

Look up the words below in your dictionary. They are from various foreign languages. Then read the definitions below the puzzle. Choose the correct word from the box to match each definition and then complete the puzzle.

obi	quoits	rutabaga	succotash
endives	rickshaw	chapeau	ascot

Across

4. a turnip with a large yellow root

6. plants related to daisies, often used in salads

7. a broad neck scarf, knotted so its ends lie flat, one on the other

8. rings tossed at a peg in a game

Down

1. a hat

2. a small, hooded carriage with two wheels that is pulled by one person

4. a stew consisting of corn, lima beans and tomatoes

5. a wide sash fastened in the back with a large, flat bow, worn in Japanese traditional dress

How Does that Sound?

A dictionary shows you not only what each word means, but also how to say it. This *pronunciation* is shown in parentheses with each word listed. A pronunciation key is listed at the beginning of the dictionary and again on each page.

Use your dictionary to find each word below and write the pronunciation for each one.

mahogany _____   strengthen _____

aardvark_____

brilliant_____

technical _____

horizon_____

exceptional _____

quiver_____

posture_____

xylophone _____

Write two of the words listed above and give the meaning for each.

1. _____

_____

2. _____

_____

Message in a Bottle

Use the pronunciation key in your dictionary to help you read the message below. Rewrite the message correctly.

Hĕlp,

Ī'm străń – dəd on ăn ī´ – lănd.

Plēz sĕnd ā bōt kwik´– lē. Ī

dōn't want tu lēv. Ī jəst nēd

ā tel´-ə- vizh -ən and ā ver´– ē

lon ĭ – lĕk – trĭ – kəl ko(ə)rd.

Sĕnd ăn īs kōld bĕv - ər – ij, tu.

Ra´– bən

One Two Three

The words below have one, two, or three syllables. Count the syllables in each word and write them in the correct column.

laugh	bases	tacks
tickle	famous	goldfish
celebrate	brisk	air
furniture	neighborhood	telescope
runway	umbrella	city
ill	butterfly	cereal
impatient	reply	earth
graph	month	canvas

one syllable	two syllables	three syllables

Dividing Words

In order to divide a word with a double consonant into syllables, you divide the word between the consonants. When the word ends in a consonant + *le*, you divide the word before the consonant. Divide the words below into syllables.

> **Example:** apple _____ap-ple_____

1. purple _____

2. bubble _____

3. trigger _____

4. butter _____

5. puzzle _____

6. turtle _____

7. fable _____

8. castle _____

9. starry _____

10. table _____

11. otter _____

12. puddle _____

13. cannon _____

14. pulley _____

15. attic _____

16. saddle _____

A Split Decision

Each of these words has a consonant sound between two vowel sounds.

- Divide a word **before** the consonant when the first vowel sound is **long**.

- Divide a word **after** the consonant when the first vowel sound is **short**.

Decide which rule to use below and circle the correct answer.

1. protect
   (prot ect) (pro tect)

2. china
   (chi na) (chin a)

3. tiger
   (tig er) (ti ger)

4. final
   (fi nal) (fin al)

5. seaport
   (seap ort) (sea port)

6. lemon
   (lem on) (le mon)

7. suburb
   (sub urb) (su burb)

8. cabin
   (cab in) (ca bin)

9. vanish
   (van ish) (va nish)

10. balance
    (ba lance) (bal ance)

11. magic
    (mag ic) (ma gic)

12. beneath
    (ben eath) (be neath)

13. human
    (hum an) (hu man)

14. level
    (lev el) (le vel)

15. sugar
    (su gar) (sug ar)

16. travel
    (tra vel) (trav el)

End of the Line

When a word won't fit on a line, you must divide it between the syllables.

| **Example:** | I left my pen- |
| | cil on my desk. |

Rewrite each word, putting one syllable on each line. Remember to use a hyphen between each syllable. Use a dictionary if you need help.

1. eyelash _____ — _____

2. slender _____ — _____

3. peaceful _____ — _____

4. balloons _____ — _____

5. willow _____ — _____

6. bathtub _____ — _____

7. saddle _____ — _____

8. zebra _____ — _____

9. chicken _____ — _____

10. raindrop _____ — _____

11. chimpanzee _____ — _____ — _____

12. yesterday _____ — _____ — _____

13. opossum _____ — _____ — _____

14. umbrella _____ — _____ — _____

15. elephant _____ — _____ — _____

16. rectangle _____ — _____ — _____

Shopping List

When a word has two or more syllables, one syllable is stressed more than the other(s). On the shopping list below, mark each stressed syllable with an accent mark ('). If the word has three or more syllables, you may need to put a secondary stress mark (''). Check your answers with a dictionary.

Example: straw' ber'' ry

1. cel   er   y

2. to   ma   to

3. pump   kins

4. ba   nan   a

5. pep   pers

6. cab   bage

7. tur   nips

8. blue   ber   ries

9. sau   sage

10. lem   on   ade

11. po   ta   toes

12. wa   ter   mel   on

13. oat   meal

14. let   tuce

15. gra   no   la

16. noo   dles

Yellow Jacket

A compound entry contains two or more words. When used together, the words have a special meaning and cannot be understood by just looking at the meaning of each word. For example, the entry "yellow jacket" is not the color of a coat, it is a type of bee.

The following word pairs are compound entries. Look them up in your dictionary and write the meaning.

1. role model _____

2. soda fountain _____

3. ghost town _____

4. goose bumps _____

5. point of view _____

6. flying saucer _____

7. leap year _____

8. boiling point _____

The following word pairs are not compound entries. Look at the meaning of each word to determine what the word pair means.

1. baseball hat _____

2. canary yellow _____

3. shower cap _____

Perfect Prefixes

Some words have prefixes. Prefixes are listed in the dictionary, but they are not whole words. If added to the beginning of a whole word, called a root word, prefixes can change the meaning of the word.

Example:	Prefix +	root word	=	new word	meaning
	un +	happy	=	unhappy	not happy

Use the dictionary to find the meaning of the prefixes below. Match the prefixes and meanings.

1. _____ anti-   A. earlier than, in front of

2. _____ tri-   B. bad or wrong

3. _____ co-   C. three

4. _____ pre-   D. opposite

5. _____ ex-   E. with, together

6. _____ mis-   F. outside, former

Now add a root word to each prefix to make a new word. Write the meaning of the new word. Use your dictionary for help.

1. tri _____ = _____

2. co _____ = _____

3. ex _____ = _____

New Meaning

Look at the prefixes and their meanings in the box. Combine these prefixes with the root words below to make new words. Write the meaning of each new word. Use a dictionary for help.

Prefix	Meaning
dis	apart from, not
auto	self
un	not
bi	two
re	again

1. _____ cycle _____

2. _____ clear _____

3. _____ pack _____

4. _____ weekly _____

5. _____ glue _____

6. _____ mobile _____

7. _____ tie _____

8. _____ obey _____

9. _____ agree _____

10. _____ locate _____

11. _____ biography _____

12. _____ arrange _____

Searching for Suffixes

Some words have suffixes. Suffixes are listed in the dictionary, but they are not whole words. If added to the end of a whole word, called a root word, they can change the meaning of the word.

Example:	Root Word	+	Suffix	=	new word	meaning
	color	+	less	=	colorless	without color

Use the dictionary to find the meaning of the suffixes below. Match the suffixes and meanings.

1. _____ -est   A. capable of, likely to

2. _____ -able, ible   B. result, goal or method

3. _____ -ment   C. state, condition

4. _____ -ous   D. most

5. _____ -ness   E. full of, having

6. _____ -ish   F. of or like

Write three words below using three of the suffixes listed above. Write the meaning of each word.

1. _____ = _____

2. _____ = _____

3. _____ = _____

Suffix Confusion

Some suffixes are spelled differently depending on the root word. Look at the root words below and decide which spelling is correct when the suffix is added. Circle the word that is spelled correctly. Use your dictionary for help.

Example: confuse
confusion
confution

1. **excel**
    excellant
    excellent

2. **complete**
    completion
    complesion

3. **accept**
    acceptable
    acceptible

4. **differ**
    differance
    difference

5. **infect**
    infectous
    infectious

6. **refer**
    referance
    reference

7. **pass**
    passible
    passable

8. **poison**
    poisonious
    poisonous

9. **expect**
    expectant
    expectent

10. **assist**
    assistance
    assistence

26

Do Your Homework

Listed with each word in the dictionary is a part of speech. Some words are listed more than once because they have more than one part of speech. The following is a list of the parts of speech you will find. The dictionary usually lists the abbreviation.

adj	adjective	*adv*	adverb
conj	conjunction	*interj*	interjection
n	noun	*prep*	preposition
pron	pronoun	*vb*	verb

Using the dictionary entries below, answer the following questions.

and (*conj*)   added to

anger (*vb*)   to make displeased

anger (*n*)   a strong feeling of displeasure

angry (*adj*)   feeling or showing anger

anyone (*pron*)   any person

1. What part of speech is *and* ? _____

   Use *and* in a sentence. _____

2. Which word is a pronoun? _____

   Use this word in a sentence. _____

   _____

3. Fill in the correct adjective. An _____ cat tore the curtains.

Decide whether the word anger is being used as a verb or a noun.

4. I will do my homework so I don't *anger* the teacher. _____

5. There was a look of *anger* on her face. _____

Under the Big Top

Locate these words in your dictionary. After each, write the part of speech: noun, verb, adjective, or adverb. Then use the word correctly in a sentence about the circus. Use your imagination and think of everything you might see under the "big top"!

1. juggled _____   _____

   _____

2. clownish _____   _____

   _____

3. vendor _____   _____

   _____

4. paraded _____   _____

   _____

5. fearlessly _____   _____

   _____

6. colorful _____   _____

   _____

7. trapeze _____   _____

   _____

8. gaily _____   _____

   _____

9. elephantine _____   _____

   _____

10. ringmaster _____   _____

   _____

Spell Check

Sometimes when you check a spelling in a dictionary, you have to look in more than one place. The beginning sounds of some words are the same although they are spelled differently. If you don't know how to spell *joy*, you might look under *g* first. Use a dictionary and complete each word correctly.

r or **rh**

1. _____ubarb

2. _____yme

3. _____oad

4. _____ode Island

5. _____uins

6. _____ifle

7. _____ino

8. _____ough

j or **g**

9. _____ ealous

10. _____ eneral

11. _____ elatin

12. _____ elly

13. _____ uicy

14. _____ umble

15. _____ enuine

16. _____ entle

How Do You Spell Funny?

Sometimes a word is not spelled exactly as it sounds. You may have to look in more than one place in your dictionary before you find it. For each word below, choose the letter or letters that will complete it correctly. Use your dictionary for help.

f or **ph**	**c** or **s**
1. _____ ase	9. _____ entence
2. _____ ate	10. _____ ement
3. _____ easant	11. _____ ircular
4. _____ rase	12. _____ ense
5. _____ loat	13. _____ ents
6. _____ inish	14. _____ elebrate
7. _____ lake	15. _____ ource
8. _____ oto	16. _____ upply

Write or Right?

Sometimes a word is not spelled exactly as it sounds. You may have to look in more than one place in your dictionary before you find it. For each word below, choose the letter or letters that will complete it correctly. Use your dictionary for help.

kn or **n**

1. _____ imble

2. _____ uckle

3. _____ eedle

4. _____ it

5. _____ eel

6. _____ ightmare

7. _____ ead

8. _____ ectar

r or **wr**

9. _____ ong

10. _____ ipen

11. _____ eaper

12. _____ estle

13. _____ ench

14. _____ ate

15. _____ eckon

16. _____ ist

Long and Short

You can find the meanings of abbreviations by looking in a dictionary. The way abbreviations are written may vary with different dictionaries. Locate each of these and write the most commonly used meaning.

1. I.O.U. _____

2. cm. _____

3. Mr. _____

4. Jan. _____

5. no. _____

6. COD _____

7. mph _____

8. hr. _____

9. Ms. _____

10. lat. _____

11. mo. _____

12. min. _____

Write three more abbreviations and their meanings.

1. _____ = _____

2. _____ = _____

3. _____ = _____

What It Stands For

An acronym is a word made from the first letters of a name. The set of letters is pronounced as a word. Locate these acronyms in a dictionary. Write out the word that each letter represents.

1. UNICEF _____

    _____

2. NOW _____

    _____

3. AWOL _____

    _____

4. RADAR _____

    _____

5. SCUBA _____

    _____

6. WAC _____

    _____

7. NASA _____

    _____

8. HUD _____

    _____

A Good Match

If you have forgotten what a synonym is, look up its meaning in the dictionary. Then look up each word below and find its synonym in the box. Write the synonym on the line.

minor	sight	real
reward	backward	carry
expanded	empty	decrease
heavy	change	damage

1. actual _____

2. alter _____

3. bonus_____

4. transport _____

5. injure _____

6. petty_____

7. vacant _____

8. swell_____

9. reduce _____

10. vision _____

11. reversed_____

12. weighty _____

Same and Different

Some words are spelled the same, but have different meanings. These words have separate entries in the dictionary. Look up each of these words in your dictionary and write the different meanings that match the part of speech.

A. match

   1. (vb) _____

   2. (n) _____

B. tear

   1. (n) _____

   2. (n) _____

   3. (vb) _____

C. plain

   1. (adj) _____

   2. (n) _____

D. bluff

   1. (n) _____

   2. (vb) _____

E. tire

   1. (vb) _____

   2. (vb) _____

Tied in Knots

Homophones are words that sound alike, but have different spellings and meanings. Below you will find a pair of homophones followed by sentences. Fill in the blank in each sentence with the correct homophone. Use your dictionary for help.

1. **piece** or **peace**

   A. Can I borrow a _____ of paper?

   B. There was finally _____ and quiet when the dog stopped barking.

2. **principle** or **principal**

   A. The _____ decided to have a school pizza party.

   B. It was a matter of _____ that she return the money she found.

3. **roll** or **role**

   A. My sister got the lead _____ in the play.

   B. I ate a delicious _____ at dinner last night.

4. **pear** or **pair**

   A. Grandma has a _____ tree in her back yard.

   B. Dad lost his favorite _____ of socks.

5. **plane** or **plain**

   A. Without the decorations, the room looked _____.

   B. They boarded the _____ 20 minutes early.

6. **reed** or **read**

   A. The _____ of grass tickled my bare feet.

   B. I _____ every night before I go to bed.

7. **scent**, **cent** or **sent**

   A. The package was _____ through the mail.

   B. The _____ helped the dog find the missing bone.

   C. I didn't spend one _____ at the mall.

Original Meaning

Etymology is the history of a word. A word's history, or origin, is what language the word was taken from and what it meant. Look up these words in your dictionary to find the information you need.

1. **jeans**   origin: _____

   what it meant: _____

   what it means: _____

   _____

2. **dime**   origin: _____

   what it meant: _____

   what it means: _____

   _____

3. **vaccine**   origin: _____

   what it meant: _____

   what it means: _____

   _____

4. **eavesdrop**   origin: _____

   what it meant: _____

   what it means: _____

   _____

5. **piano**   origin: _____

   what it meant: _____

   what it means: _____

Bird or Beast

Many dictionaries include pictures, or *illustrations*, to help you understand definitions. Find each word below in your dictionary and write in the blank whether it is a *bird* or a *beast*. Then describe what it looks like.

Bird or Beast

1. **oryx:** _____

   Description: _____

2. **emu:** _____

   Description: _____

3. **auk:** _____

   Description: _____

4. **lemur:** _____

   Description : _____

5. **ptarmigan:** _____

   Description: _____

6. **marabou:** _____

   Description: _____

7. **pangolin:** _____

   Description: _____

8. **hornbil:** _____

   Description: _____

Internet Dictionary Overview

A dictionary in book form is called a **bound** dictionary. There are also dictionaries on the Internet. A dictionary found on the Internet may look a little different, but you can use it for all the same reasons you would use a bound version.

- ## Why would I use an Internet dictionary?

    Internet dictionaries are easy and quick to use, especially when you are already working on the computer. They can also contain more information than a bound dictionary.

    Abridged dictionaries reduced in length, or cut short. *Unabridged* dictionaries contain original content, and are not cut short. Internet dictionaries are unabridged. They can contain endless amounts of the most current information. Bound dictionaries can only be so big and when changes are made, or words added, a whole new set of books needs to be printed.

- ## What are some Internet dictionary sites?

    Have a parent or teacher help you go to a search engine and type in keywords such as **dictionary** or **online dictionary**. The following is a short list of Internet dictionaries you may find:

    http://www.m-w.com

    http://education.yahoo.com/reference/dictionary

    http://www.dictionary.com

    http://www.factmonster.com/dictionary.html

- ## How do I use an Internet dictionary?

    All of the sites look a little different, and sometimes a site changes the way it looks. Most sites will have a box for you to enter a word for which to search. Some will have a help section. Most sites will help you find a word even if your spelling is wrong, and once a word is found, most sites will show the definition, pronunciation (some sites will pronounce the word for you), syllabication, and maybe even an illustration or word history.

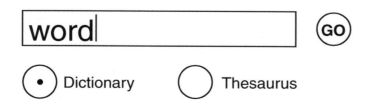

Fact Finder

Go to an Internet dictionary such as **www.m-w.com**. Use this dictionary to answer the questions below.

1. What are two definitions for *earwig*?

   A. (n) _____

   B. (v) _____

2. Write the definition for the following three words.

   A. aspire_____

   B. expire_____

   C. perspire _____

3. Use the word *earsplitting* in a sentence. _____

4. Use the word *obvious* in a sentence. _____

For #5–8, find the information needed for each word.

5. **humorous**

   A. Definition: _____

   B. Pronunciation: _____   C. Part of Speech: _____

6. **humerus**

   A. Definition: _____

   B. Pronunciation: _____   C. Part of Speech: _____

7. **designated hitter**

   A. Definition: _____

   B. Abbreviation: _____   C. Part of Speech: _____

8. **mesa**

   A. Definition: _____

   B. Etymology:_____

Versatile Vocabulary

Below you will find groups of four words followed by four sentences. Look up the words on an Internet dictionary. Then, use them to correctly complete the sentences that follow.

hypocrite	sociable
antisocial	sincere

1. The _____ told me to quiet down even though he was very loud.

2. My _____ neighbor never even says hello.

3. When I saw how embarrassed she was, I knew her apology was _____.

4. The _____ new student made friends quickly.

tattered	rejuvenated
piercing	tranquil

5. A good movie, dark room and cozy blanket made him feel _____.

6. My grandmother's old, _____ diary was a joy to read.

7. A cold glass of lemonade _____ me on that hot day.

8. The _____ crash sent a shiver up my spine.

lethargic	chivalrous
uncouth	magnificent

9. The _____ boy gave her his coat when she looked cold.

10. The city lights looked _____ as we eagerly approached.

11. People who talk all the way through a movie are very _____.

12. Her bad cold made her feel _____ and weak.

Unit Assessment

Read each question carefully. Mark the best answer. Fill in the bubble completely. You may use your dictionary.

1. Which of these word groups is in alphabetical order?
   - Ⓐ feet, read, team
   - Ⓑ tree, grass, flow
   - Ⓒ stand, and, band
   - Ⓓ tag, frog, bat

2. Which of these word groups is in alphabetical order?
   - Ⓐ small, set, soft
   - Ⓑ mask, move, melt
   - Ⓒ gem, give, great
   - Ⓓ pour, pull price

3. Which of these word groups is in alphabetical order?
   - Ⓐ leap, lean, leak
   - Ⓑ rock, roll, role
   - Ⓒ trip, trim, trick
   - Ⓓ base, bath, bay

4. The guide words on the dictionary page are *branch* and *brick*. Which word would **not** be found on that page?
   - Ⓐ breath
   - Ⓑ break
   - Ⓒ brief
   - Ⓓ bribe

5. The guide words on the dictionary page are *right* and *robot*. Which word would **not** be found on that page?
   - Ⓐ rival
   - Ⓑ rift
   - Ⓒ roast
   - Ⓓ robin

6. The guide words on the dictionary page are *skim* and *sled*. Which word would **not** be found on that page?
   - Ⓐ skill
   - Ⓑ slap
   - Ⓒ skull
   - Ⓓ slant

7. Which of these is the correct phonetic spelling for *quiet* ?
   - Ⓐ kw–ī ət
   - Ⓑ kwī-ət
   - Ⓒ qw–ī ət
   - Ⓓ qwī-ət

8. Which of these is the correct phonetic spelling for *phobia*?
   - Ⓐ fō-bē-ə
   - Ⓑ fō-bē-a
   - Ⓒ fō-bī-ə
   - Ⓓ phō-bē-ə

Unit Assessment *(cont.)*

For #9–12, choose the correct way to divide the following words into syllables.

9. turtle

    Ⓐ tu rtle   Ⓒ tur tle

    Ⓑ turt le   Ⓓ t urtle

10. ferry

    Ⓐ fe rry   Ⓒ ferr y

    Ⓑ f erry   Ⓓ fer ry

11. modern

    Ⓐ mode rn   Ⓒ mo dern

    Ⓑ m odern   Ⓓ mod ern

12. patient

    Ⓐ pat ient   Ⓒ patie nt

    Ⓑ pa tient   Ⓓ pati ent

13. Which is the meaning for the prefix *un-*?

    Ⓐ again   Ⓒ self

    Ⓑ not   Ⓓ opposite

14. Which is the meaning for the prefix *tri-*?

    Ⓐ earlier   Ⓒ three

    Ⓑ two   Ⓓ one

15. Which is the meaning for the prefix *anti-*?

    Ⓐ opposite   Ⓒ again

    Ⓑ wrong   Ⓓ apart from

16. Which is the meaning for the prefix *pre-*?

    Ⓐ before   Ⓒ three

    Ⓑ opposite   Ⓓ after

Unit Assessment *(cont.)*

17. Which is the meaning for the suffix –*able*?
     Ⓐ capable of   Ⓒ most
     Ⓑ result   Ⓓ full of

18. Which is the meaning for the suffix –*est*?
     Ⓐ like   Ⓒ full of
     Ⓑ state   Ⓓ most

19. Which is the meaning for the suffix –*ish*?
     Ⓐ like   Ⓑ most
     Ⓒ capable of   Ⓓ result

For #20-22, choose the part of speech for the underlined word.

20. The cat <u>meowed</u> all night.
     Ⓐ noun   Ⓑ verb
     Ⓒ adjective   Ⓓ adverb

21. Her <u>purple</u> hat blew away with the wind.
     Ⓐ noun   Ⓑ adjective
     Ⓒ adverb   Ⓓ preposition

22. The bird sat quietly <u>on</u> the boat.
     Ⓐ interjection   Ⓑ preposition
     Ⓒ adverb   Ⓓ verb

23. Which spelling is the correct way to complete the word _____ yme?
     Ⓐ rh   Ⓑ r

24. Which spelling is the correct way to complete the word _____ entle?
     Ⓐ j   Ⓑ g

25. Which spelling is the correct way to complete the word _____ easant?
     Ⓐ ph   Ⓑ f

Unit Assessment *(cont.)*

26. Which spelling is the correct way to complete the word _____ightmare?

Ⓐ kn
Ⓑ n

27. Which word is a synonym for *humble*?

Ⓐ small   Ⓒ silly
Ⓑ huge   Ⓓ modest

28. Which word is a synonym for *lethargic*?

Ⓐ long   Ⓒ inactive
Ⓑ busy   Ⓓ energetic

For #29-32, choose the correct word to complete the sentence.

29. He _____ the teacher say the test was postponed.

Ⓐ herd   Ⓑ heard

30. The girl lost a _____ on her bike when she fell.

Ⓐ pedal   Ⓑ peddle

31. The man hit his _____ when the light turned red.

Ⓐ brake   Ⓑ break

32. The _____ of flowers was overwhelming.

Ⓐ sent   Ⓑ scent

33. His _____ arm throbbed all day.

Ⓐ sore   Ⓑ soar

34. There was a beautiful _____ running through the meadow.

Ⓐ creek   Ⓑ creak

Answer Key

Page 5
1. animal
2. beach
3. caterpillar
4. drawer
5. eyelash
6. flashlight
7. grill
8. helmet
9. iguana
10. jewel
11. kingdom
12. lilac
13. maple
14. noun
15. otter
16. paragraph
17. quarter
18. radish
19. sidewalk
20. toad
21. unicorn
22. vegetable
23. water
24. xylophone
25. yellow
26. zipper

Page 6
1. canary
2. crow
3. eagle
4. egret
5. finch
6. flamingo
7. oriole
8. osprey
9. peacock
10. pigeon
11. seagull
12. starling

Page 7
1. aunt
2. author
3. blaze
4. block
5. blue
6. gadget
7. game
8. garage
9. jam
10. jar
11. money
12. motor
13. raft
14. rain
15. ranger
16. stamp
17. steam
18. straw
19. wolf
20. wood

Page 8
Answers will vary.

Page 9
1. touch
2. toucan
3. 756
4. 755
5.–6. Answers will vary.

Page 10
1. fly
2. much
3. color
4. left
5. need
6. gnu
7. reading
8. heel
9. bird
10. giraffe
11. click
12. dice

Page 11

call/cap
calves
camel
candle
canopy

cheap/chemical
cheat
check
cheetah
chef

cow/cream
cowboy
coy
crab
cracker

cold/comment
colony
color
combine
comic

Page 12
Answers will vary according to dictionary used.

Page 13
Answers will vary slightly.
1. piece of gymnasium equipment
2. understanding
3. chimney
4. indent, hollow place
5. sad
6. grumpy person

Page 14
Across

Page 15
məhŏgᵊ ne
ärd´värk
tĕk´ni kəl
ik sĕp´shənəl
pŏs´chər
strĕngk´thən
bril´yənt
hərī´zən
kwiv´ər
zī´ləfon
1.–2. Answers will vary.

Page 16
Help,
I'm stranded on an island.
Please send a boat quickly. I
don't want to leave. I just need
a television and a very
long electrical cord.
Send an ice cold beverage, too.
Robin

Page 17
One Syllable
laugh
ill
graph
brisk

month
tack
air
earth

Two Syllables
tickle
runway
bases
famous
reply
goldfish
city
canvas

Three Syllables
celebrate
furniture
impatient
neighborhood
umbrella
butterfly
telescope
cereal

Page 18
1. pur-ple
2. bub-ble
3. trig-ger
4. but-ter
5. puz-zle
6. tur-tle
7. fa-ble
8. cas-tle
9. star-ry
10. ta-ble
11. ot-ter
12. pud-dle
13. can-non
14. pul-ley
15. at-tic
16. sad-dle

Page 19
1. pro tect
2. chi na
3. ti ger
4. fi nal
5. sea port
6. lem on
7. sub urb
8. cab in
9. van ish
10. bal ance
11. mag ic
12. be neath
13. hu man
14. lev el
15. sug ar
16. trav el

Answer Key *(cont.)*

Page 20
1. eye-lash
2. slen-der
3. peace-ful
4. bal-loons
5. wil-low
6. bath-tub
7. sad-dle
8. ze-bra
9. chick-en
10. rain-drop
11. chim-pan-zee
12. yes-ter-day
13. o-pos-sum
14. um-brel-la
15. el-e-phant
16. rec-tan-gle

Page 21
1. cel´ er y
2. to ma´ to
3. pump´ kins
4. ba nan´ a
5. pep´ pers
6. cab´ bage
7. tur´ nips
8. blue´ ber´´ ry
9. sau´ sage
10. lem on ade´
11. po ta´ toes
12. wa´ ter mel´´ on
13. oat´ meal
14. let´ tuce
15. gra no´ la
16. noo´ dles

Page 22
Answers will vary slightly.
1. person who serves as model to emulate
2. counter where soft drinks/ice cream are served
3. deserted town
4. rough skin caused by cold, fear, excitement
5. a way of looking at/thinking about something
6. unidentified flying object
7. a year with 366 days; has February 29
8. temperature at which liquid boils
1. a hat worn in baseball
2. yellow like a canary
3. a cap worn in the shower

Page 23
1. D
2. C
3. E
4. A
5. F
6. B
1–3. Answers will vary.

Page 24
Answers may vary.

Page 25
1. D
2. A
3. B
4. E
5. C
6. F
1.–3. Answers will vary.

Page 26
1. excellent
2. completion
3. acceptable
4. difference
5. infectious
6. reference
7. passable
8. poisonous
9. expectant
10. assistance

Page 27
1. conjunction (sentence will vary)
2. anyone (sentence will vary)
3. angry
4. verb
5. noun

Page 28
Sentences will vary.
1. verb
2. adjective
3. noun
4. verb
5. adverb
6. adjective
7. noun
8. adverb
9. adjective
10. noun

Page 29
1. rhubarb
2. rhyme
3. road
4. Rhode Island
5. ruins
6. rifle
7. rhino

8. rough
9. jealous
10. general
11. gelatin
12. jelly
13. juicy
14. jumble
15. genuine
16. gentle

Page 30
1. phase
2. fate
3. pheasant
4. phrase
5. float
6. finish
7. flake
8. photo
9. sentence
10. cement
11. circular
12. sense
13. cents
14. celebrate
15. source
16. supply

Page 31
1. nimble
2. knuckle
3. needle
4. knit
5. kneel
6. nightmare
7. knead
8. nectar
9. wrong
10. ripen
11. reaper
12. wrestle
13. wrench
14. rate
15. reckon
16. wrist

Page 32
1. written promise to pay a debt
2. centimeter
3. Mister
4. January
5. north
6. cash on delivery
7. miles per hour
8. hour
9. Miss
10. latitude
11. month
12. minute

Answer Key (cont.)

1.–3. Answers will vary.

Page 33
1. United Nations International Children's Emergency Fund
2. National Organization for Women
3. absent without leave
4. radio detecting and ranging
5. self-contained underwater breathing apparatus
6. Women's Army Corps
7. National Aeronautics and Space Administration
8. Department of Housing and Urban Development

Page 34
1. real
2. change
3. reward
4. carry
5. damage
6. minor
7. empty
8. expanded
9. decrease
10. sight
11. backward
12. heavy

Page 35
Answers may vary.

Page 36
1. A. piece   B. peace
2. A. principal B. principle
3. A. role   B. roll
4. A. pear   B. pair
5. A. plain   B. plane
6. A. reed   B. read
7. A. sent   B. scent
   C. cent

Page 37
1. **origin:** English
   what it meant: sturdy cotton cloth
   what it means: pants made of heavy cotton cloth
2. **origin:** French and/or Latin
   what it meant: tenth part
   what it means: US coins worth ten cents
3. **origin:** Latin
   what it meant: cow
   what it means: a material used to protect against disease

4. **origin:** English
   what it meant: the ground on which water fell from a house
   what it means: secretly listen to a private conversation
5. **origin:** Italian
   what it meant: soft and loud
   what it means: a keyboard instrument

Page 38
Answers will vary slightly.
1. beast—antelope, long horns, hump above shoulders
2. bird—large, resembles ostrich, doesn't fly
3. bird—chunky body, webbed feet, short wings
4. beast—large eyes, long muzzle, long tail
5. bird—feathered legs or feet, brown or gray
6. bird—stork, white down on underside
7. beast—long tail, scales, long snout, sticky tongue
8. bird—large bill with bump at the base

Page 40
Answers may vary slightly.
1. A. insect with pincher-like appendages
   B. to annoy or influence with confidential talk
2. A. to seek to accomplish a particular goal
   B. to come to an end
   C. to secrete and emit
3. Answers will vary.
4. Answers will vary.
5. A. full of or showing humor
   B. hyoo m r s
   C. adjective ə ə
6. A. bone in arm extending from shoulder to elbow
   B. hyoo m r s
   C. noun´ ə ə
7. A. a baseball player who bats instead of a pitcher
   B. DH
   C. noun
8. A. broad, plat-topped elevation with cliff-like sides
   B. Spanish, meaning table

Page 41
1. hypocrite
2. antisocial
3. sincere
4. sociable
5. tranquil
6. tattered
7. rejuvenated
8. piercing
9. chivalrous
10. magnificent
11. uncouth
12. lethargic

Page 42
1. A
2. C
3. D
4. C
5. B
6. A
7. B
8. A

Page 43
9. C
10. D
11. D
12. B
13. B
14. C
15. A
16. A

Page 44
17. A
18. D
19. A
20. B
21. B
22. B
23. A
24. B
25. A

Page 45
26. B
27. D
28. C
29. B
30. A
31. A
32. B
33. A
34. A